IMAGES
of America

JOHNSTON

The Hurricane Riders, a Johnston club of serious motorcycle riders, was formed after Hurricane Carol in 1954. The group met at various sites in town. From left to right are (front row) Tuffy Acciardo (president), Rip Horman (vice president), Ric Forcino (secretary), and Don McAllister (treasurer); (second row) unknown, Freddy Macari, George Gesmondi, and Abby Macari; (third row) Vern Whitaker, ? Stanley, Joe Tartaglia, Walter Kimball, and unknown; (back row) Flukey Stanley, Peter Jacavone, unknown, ? Brown, and unknown. (Photograph courtesy of Don McAllister.)

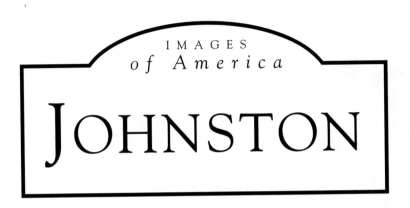

IMAGES
of America

JOHNSTON

Louis H. McGowan
and the Johnston Historical Society

ARCADIA

Published by Arcadia Publishing,
an imprint of the Chalford Publishing Corporation,
One Washington Center, Dover, New Hampshire 03820.
Printed in Great Britain

Library of Congress Cataloging-in-Publication Data applied for

These four Johnston Historical Society officers put together this book. They spent many hours getting together with Johnston residents to look over old photographs and to listen to tales of the old days. From left to right are (front) Steve Merolla and Pat Macari; (back) Louis McGowan and Dan Brown. (Photograph by Nancy Brown.)

Contents

The 1961 All-Star Team from the Johnston Teener League, a nationwide VFW-sponsored system, is shown here. The Ciarlo-LaPrade Post sponsored the local league. Four teams represented Thornton, Manton, Graniteville, and Winsor Hill. Pictured from left to right are (front row) Tony D'uva, Vin Ascenzi, David Bolton, David Rioles, Hank Konerko, Ted LaChance, Bob Scott, and Alex Giarrusso; (back row) Coach Tom Cappelli, Bob Girasole, Jim Petterutti, Louis McGowan, Al Lisi, Mike Valois, Benny Coletta, Tom Donnelly, Manager Leo Kennedy, and Coach Bob Smith. The batboy is Bill Caito.

Acknowledgments

The Johnston Historical Society would like to thank the many people who contributed their time, knowledge of the town, and precious family photographs for this book. Not every photograph could be fit into the book because of space limitations, but photo-grade copies were made of every picture given to us. These copies and the originals donated to the society are now on file at the JHS headquarters, where they will be preserved as part of the historical record of the town. The society will continue to collect photographs for this collection, which can be viewed by the general public. The Johnston Historical Society is located at 101 Putnam Pike. Our telephone number is (401) 231-3380.

Our thanks go to the following people for donating photographs and/or historical information: Mabel Atwood Sprague, Mario Votolato, Anthony Rainone, Charles Redinger, Mike Placella, Clara Mills, Lora Clemence, Herb Newman, Elaine Mathewson Pereira, Mike Hebert, Lou Ullucci, Irving Almonte, Anne Parrillo, Sam and Lillian Coupe, Joe Uciffero, Mary Carroll, the Russo family, the D'Acchioli family, Whytebrook Terrace, Walter Nebiker, Mohr Library, Gina Perrotta, Anna Armstrong, Henry Armstrong, Mike Rossi, Earl Blamires, Mr. and Mrs. Harold Beaudoin, Vin Crosby, Donald Catley, Albert Wood, Arthur Harrington, Bob Jackson, George Dansereau, Nellie Dahlin, Kevin Neel, Al Kimball, Connie Ricci, Manton Hose Co. #3, Joe Coduri, Hede Aurecchia, Phyllis Ferruolo, John Mancini, Phil Paige, the Belknap family, Scott Molloy, Richard DelFino, Dorothy Ferri Willner, Ernie Marchetti, John Negris, John Rossi, Rich LaFazia, Jim Goss, Lou DelFino, Lennie Macari, Fred Corcoran, Evelyn Beaumier, Carol Pace, Ace Cappelli, Carolyn Thornton, Bob Larivee, and Tom Greene.

Introduction

The area encompassed by present-day Johnston was part of Providence until 1759. In March of 1759, a petition to the state general assembly was granted for the creation of the Town of Johnston. The residents of western Providence had opted for this petition because they did not like traveling so far to town meetings. The new town was named after Augustus Johnston, a very popular Rhode Island attorney general. Ironically, he was later driven from the state for remaining loyal to the Crown.

For its first fifty years Johnston remained a quiet, agricultural town. Other than farms, only the occasional gristmill, sawmill, blacksmith shop, or wheelwright shop dotted the landscape. An exception was an early rolling and slitting mill built in 1788 in Olneyville and run by Christopher Olney. The textile industry in Johnston also started in the same village in 1808 with the Union Mill. Soon mills sprouted up in Merino, Simmonsville, Simmons Lower Village, Morgan Mills, Hughesdale, and Caesarville. Mills in the North Providence villages of Greystone and Centerdale also provided work for Johnston residents. The mills contributed to the growth of most of eastern Johnston, while the western half remained rural.

By the late eighteenth century the industrial age had begun and better roads were needed. Up to that point local residents took care of roads in their own highway district by contributing money and labor. The system did not work all that well, and private revenue-producing companies were therefore given a chance. Four turnpikes, each charging tolls for part of their length, ran through Johnston. The first to be operated was the Plainfield Pike, or the Providence and Norwich Turnpike, chartered in 1794. It ran from Olneyville, across Johnston. The Hartford Pike, or the Rhode Island and Connecticut Turnpike, was chartered in 1803 and ran from Olneyville across the town. A tollhouse stood just west of Shang Bailey's roadhouse in the western part of Johnson. The Powder Mill Turnpike, today's Putnam Pike, was opened in 1815 and ran across the northeast corner of the town. The Central Pike was chartered in 1822 as the Foster and Scituate Turnpike, but came to be called by its present name because of its location between the Hartford and Plainfield Pikes. If a traveler wanted to avoid the tolls, he took the Shun Pike or else the Free Pike (today's Scituate Avenue).

Travel on dirt roads presented obvious problems. The railroad came to Olneyville by the 1830s and to Manton and Graniteville in 1873. Four different trolley lines served the town. Two lines were run by the Union Railroad (later the Rhode Island Company), one going from Olneyville out Plainfield Street to Thornton and then to Hughesdale. The second line ran out Greenville Avenue to Manton from Olneyville. The Providence and Danielson Railroad also operated two lines that went through town. One ran up Smith Street to Graniteville and on to Chepachet. A second line traveled along the Hartford Road across the town. These steam and electric railroads helped to: (1) promote economic and housing growth; (2) enable workers to reach factories; and (3) bring goods back and forth to rural areas.

The trolley opened up Thornton for modern, large textile mills. The British Hosiery Mill opened in 1884 with a full complement of workers from the old country. The Victoria Mill and the Pocasset Worsted Mill commenced operations in 1898, and soon 1,200 people found work in the Thornton mills. When the west Olneyville section of Johnston was annexed back to Providence in 1898, the town hall and police station moved from Olneyville to Thornton, which was rapidly developing. The annexation cut Johnston's population from 11,200 to 4,300 in one big slice, and the town did not recover this loss until well into the twentieth century.

The mills in Thornton continued to operate during the twentieth century, some making it to the 1950s. In Johnston's other villages, the mills were mostly silent by the 1920s. Hughesdale, Simmonsville, Morgan Mills, and Caesarville had all stopped producing textiles. Farming continued to dominate in the West End and rail travel disappeared as the auto age progressed. Only the old Providence & Springfield Railroad, bought by the New York, New Haven, and Hartford Railroad in 1905, made it past the 1930s, by which time it no longer carried passengers. It ceased running in 1962.

One important shift in the ethnic background of the town's population occurred in the late nineteenth century. Until that time, people of English and Irish background made up most of the town's population. In the 1870s and 1880s Italian immigrants started settling in the town, working on farms in Pocasset and Simmonsville. By the early twentieth century many Italians were finding work in the textile mills and, when able to save enough money, they bought up farms along Plainfield Pike, in Simmonsville, and in Hughesdale. Soon they were providing fresh vegetables, flowers, and cider to the rapidly expanding populace of metropolitan Providence. Johnston's Italian-American population grew to the point that, in 1970, it had the highest percentage in the state of people of first- or second-generation Italian ancestry.

Johnston's school system did not get into full swing until the 1820s. Only one school is known to have existed before that time, the Belknap School. It dated from 1790 and was financed by subscribers. In the 1820s the school district system was started. Eventually sixteen districts were formed. Johnston's first high school, built in the 1880s, was in the annex area. After losing this school to Providence in 1898, Johnston had no high school until 1960. Today there are six elementary schools, one middle school, and one high school.

Johnston's spiritual needs were well taken care of, starting with the Reverend Samuel Winsor's first Baptist Meeting House in Belknap in 1771. Shortly after this was established, a second meetinghouse was built on Plainfield Street near the present St. Anthony's Church in what is now Providence. A third Baptist church was built in Manton in 1842 near the future train station. St. Peter's Episcopal Church started in a wooden building on Killingly Street in 1846. The Graniteville Baptist Church held its first meeting in the present building in 1859. Antioch's first chapel was erected in 1891, with services held in the old school before that. Hughesdale's chapel was present by 1870. The first Roman Catholic churches were St. Rocco's in 1903 and St. Brigid's in 1914, both in Thornton, and Our Lady of Grace, in Manton, in 1912.

Town meetings were held in private homes until the first Town House was built in 1842 in Pocasset village. In the last three decades of the nineteenth century, town meetings were held and town offices were located in Olneyville. From 1870 to 1885 the town hall was located in the Irons Block in Olneyville Square. By 1879 the Olneyville Free Library and Reading Room was also located in the Irons Block and later moved to a new building across the square. From 1886 to 1898 the Odd Fellows Hall at 161 Plainfield Street housed the town hall and police department. Following the annexation, the town hall, the police headquarters, and the jail moved to Thornton at 1343 Plainfield Street. In 1933 they all moved to the new town hall at Atwood and Hartford Avenues. In 1966 a new police and fire complex was built, while in 1978 the police department moved to a new building at Cherry Hill Road and Atwood Avenue.

After the annexation, bridewells (jails) were listed as being located in Thornton and Manton. The Thornton bridewell was the main jail. The Manton bridewell was located in a coal shed owned by the Newman family off Greenville Avenue from 1898 until at least 1921.

The first fire station, built in 1891 and run by volunteers, was located in Olneyville on Plainfield Street. Volunteer groups existed in Manton, Graniteville, and Thornton at that time without permanent stations. Manton Hose Company #3 built their fire barn in 1911. Thornton and Graniteville followed soon after. The West End did not have a fire station until 1953.

The rich history of Johnson is well documented in these photographs, which present and past town residents have so graciously allowed us to copy. This compilation packages what we feel will be a lasting legacy of Johnson history.

One

Thornton

Thornton, initially called Simmons Lower Village or Lower Simmonsville, saw its first settler about 1655, when Captain Arthur Fenner built his home on the Cranston side of Thornton. In 1677 his son, Major Thomas Fenner, built in the same area. Both farms included land that today is part of Johnston. Cranston and Johnston still share the village, with Plainfield Street being the dividing line. All of the mills and most of the schools and churches were on the Johnston side, however.

A gristmill, a machine shop, and a blacksmith shop, all belonging to the Fenner family, were present along Cedar Swamp Brook in the 1820s, and textile manufacturing started in the 1830s. Modern growth began with the erection of the British Hosiery Mill in 1884. In the last decade of the nineteenth century, the Pocasset Worsted Mill and Victoria Mill were built, the village was re-named Thornton, and trolley rails were run up Plainfield Street. After the Olneyville-Silver Lake section was annexed to Providence in 1898, the town hall and police station moved to Thornton, which truly became the center of life in town. Since then, the textile mills have closed, the town hall has re-located, and commercial activity has lessened, but the village remains a vital part of the town.

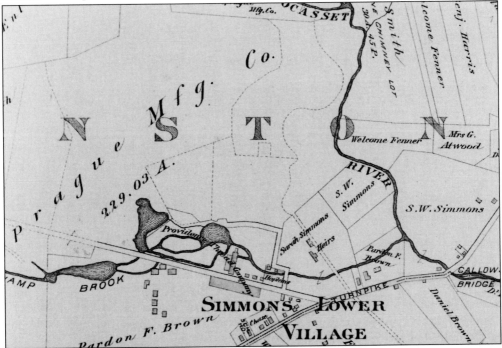

This 1882 map of Thornton shows how little development there was in the village at that time. Within thirty years, new large mills and the trolley would help greatly to change the landscape.

Located on Plainfield Street along the Pocasset River, the Brown Mill was built probably in 1832 by Pardon Fenner. Textiles were made here from that time until the middle of the twentieth century. Some firms doing business here were Daniel Brown, mid-nineteenth century; Pocasset Warp Co., 1890s; Samuel Fitch Co. , 1900s; National Silk Hosiery Co., 1910s-1920s; Pettaconsett Mfg. Co., 1920s; and Tabco Braid Co., 1950s and 1960s. (Photograph courtesy of Mabel Sprague.)

This c. 1915 postcard view of the Simmons Mansion shows part of the landscaped gardens reaching to Plainfield Pike. James F. Simmons, a wealthy mill owner and U.S. Senator, had this mansion built about 1840 probably by Russell Warren. Two other mill owners lived here after him, a Mr. Dugdale of the Thornton Worsted Mill and Robert W. Cooper of the British Hosiery Mill.

The British Hosiery Mill, shown in this *c.* 1910 view, was built in 1884 by Charles Fletcher for Robert W. Cooper. In that year Cooper moved here from England with his knitting machines and 120 English workers. They produced knitted cashmere hosiery, which began a new industry in this country. In the 1910s and 1920s George E. Boyden ran the mill. From the 1920s until the early 1950s Priscilla Worsted Company operated here, followed by Barker Chadsey, which closed in 1982.

Robert W. Cooper was a hosiery maker in his native England. Unable to tap the large U.S. market for fancy men's socks because of restrictive tariffs, he decided to move to America. With his mill ready for him in Thornton, he commenced production of socks in 1884. He contributed much to his workers' lives, including sports, dance groups, literary groups, and a brass band.

This *c.* 1910 postcard view shows the Johnston side of Plainfield Street, looking east from Atwood Avenue. The first five buildings in the foreground are all gone, including what appears to be a late-eighteenth-century house, probably belonging to the Brown family, fourth from the left. No automobiles are present, and horse-drawn vehicles were still the main means of everyday transport.

This early-twentieth-century photograph shows the interior of Hartshorn's Bar on Plainfield Street, which later became Ferri's Tavern. Second from the left is Thomas Hartshorn, the owner; third from the left is Samuel J. Coupe; on the right is Fannie Hartshorn, Thomas' wife, who cooked and served food. (Photograph courtesy of Samuel Coupe.)

John Votolato, friend to the Italian-American community and strong businessman, is shown in this advertisement from a 1910 Johnston Directory. His varied skills were used to help newcomers from Italy adjust to life here. He was the first Italo-American to serve on the town council. His son, Mario, still runs a flag store in Myrtle Hall on Plainfield Street. (Photograph courtesy of Mario Votolato.)

Thornton Hardware was run by John (Giovanni) Votolato and his wife Pasqualena. This c. 1915 photograph shows Pasqualena, her son Vincent, and her daughter, Virginia. At this time the store was located one block west of Myrtle Hall. Later John purchased the Myrtle Hall building and moved the store there. (Photograph courtesy of Mario Votolato.)

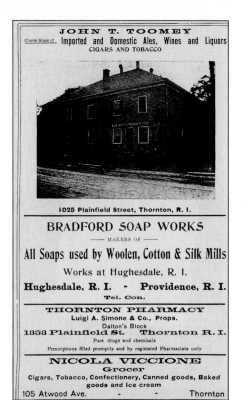

This 1913 Johnston Directory advertisement shows John Toomey's Liquor and Cigar Store at 1025 Plainfield Street. It was located on the site of Fenner's Tavern (also Fenner's Stand), a famous nightspot that was built by 1851. The 1025 Banquet Hall is now at this site. The bottom two advertisements reflect the rising presence of Italian businessmen in Thornton.

Francesco Iannuccilli stands in front of his grocery store at 1451 Plainfield Street at the corner of John Street about 1919. Items in the window include lava soap, canned goods, dry and fresh vegetables, and milk. In the pre-supermarket days, small markets like these were located every couple of blocks in built-up areas. (Photograph courtesy of Hede Aurrechia.)

This 1926 photograph looks east on Plainfield Street over the Thornton Bridge. The Brown Mill peeks out at the left and the trolley tracks are seen in the center of the street. All the buildings in the scene are in Johnston except for the one on the right. For many years the bridge was known as Gallows Bridge. (Photograph courtesy of RIDOT.)

The Thornton Bridge, or Gallows Bridge as it was known for many years, spans the Pocasset River where it crosses Plainfield Street. How it acquired this latter name is unknown. The colorful explanation is that a hanging or hangings took place here. The picturesque stone arch bridge, shown in this 1913 photograph, still spans the river, a graphic reminder of old-time craftsmanship. The building on the right was actually in Cranston, the river being the town line. (Photograph courtesy of RIDOT.)

This 1928 photograph looks east along Atwood Avenue toward Plainfield Street. The Ferri Block is the long building on the right. The workers are repairing the Atwood Avenue Bridge, which spans Cedar Swamp Brook, a tributary of the Pocasset River. A trolley waits to pass the bridge on its way to Hughesdale. (Photograph courtesy of RIDOT.)

Tracks were laid to Thornton in the 1880s for use with horse-drawn trolleys. Later, electric trolleys of the Union Railroad were used on this line. Charles Fletcher, who built the three largest mills in Thornton, was instrumental in securing this service for the village. The trolleys brought workers from Olneyville to his Thornton mills, supplementing his workforce. The early-twentieth-century trolley pictured here ran to Hughesdale.

Plainfield Pike had its origins in the Great North Road, which was laid out by the state in 1714. The road probably followed an earlier path, though, since houses were already constructed along this route in the seventeenth century. From 1794 to the early years of the 1800s, the Providence and Norwich Turnpike followed this path. With the coming of automobiles, more modern roads were needed, and hence the work in this 1911 postcard scene. (Photograph courtesy of Evelyn Beaumier.)

Looking past Benny Ricci's gas station, this 1935 photograph shows the Ferri Block across Atwood Avenue. The men pictured are, from left to right, Bennie Ricci, Lou Petrucci, and Carl Petronio. Many different businesses were located in the Ferri building, including Emil Fuoco's Spa, a pool hall, a bowling alley, and a movie theater. Before the theater was installed, there was a hall on the second floor where roller skating took place and functions such as weddings were held. (Photograph courtesy of Connie Ricci.)

A native of England, Charles Fletcher was a textile giant in Rhode Island in the late nineteenth and early twentieth century. He had a profound influence in Johnston, building the town's three largest mills. To facilitate the running of these mills, he was instrumental in having a section of Plainfield Street built between Morgan Avenue and School Street. Avoiding the steep grade on Morgan Avenue, the trolleys were able to run smoothly along the new section of Plainfield Street.

The Victoria Mill, shown in this c. 1915 postcard view, was built by Charles Fletcher for his son-in-law, Harry Hartley. Located on Mill Street near the site of the 1830 Bag Mill, this mill under Hartley produced washed, scoured, and combed raw wool until going bankrupt in 1931. The Berker Machine Company and the American Foam Company have occupied the complex since 1941.

Johnston Police Chief Hiram Kimball is shown on his horse leading a parade on John Street in the Frog City section of Thornton. The Victoria Mill looms in the background. The parade was probably part of Saint Rocco's feast and dates to the early twentieth century.

This *c.* 1910 view shows Benny Ricci with his mother, Nicoline, and his father, Luigi, in front of their house on Mill Street at the corner of Baker Street. The small grocery store at the left was owned by Mr. Ricci and served the workers at Victoria Mill, located just up the street. (Photograph courtesy of Connie Ricci.)

This bird's-eye view shows the Pocasset Worsted Mill, constructed by Charles Fletcher in 1898, before the north wing of the mill was built. Owned and operated by Fletcher, the Pocasset Street mill employed up to one thousand workers. Forty-one duplex mill houses, shown on the right, were built on adjoining streets. The Walter Marshall Spinning Company ran the mill from the mid-1930s to 1968. The mill was also responsible for the Pocasset Casino and the nearby soccer/cricket field.

William Gill, superintendent of the Pocasset Worsted Mill from the 1910s until the mid-1930s when the mill closed, lived in the superintendent's house across from the Pocasset Casino on Plainfield Street. Pictured here in the mill he was a very popular man and served as chairman of the school committee for a number of years.

The Pocasset Casino or Pocasset Social Club was built in the early twentieth century for the workers at the Pocasset Worsted Mill. The building at 1192 Plainfield Street housed bowling alleys, pool tables, banquet rooms, and a stage. Extensively used by village members, it was sold to the Sons of Italy in 1928, a group of Italian businessmen from the area. The club burned in 1944 and was replaced by the present structure.

Like many textile mills around Rhode Island, the Pocasset Worsted Mill provided housing for many of its workers. This 1903 view from a state report shows worker housing on Maple Avenue near the mill. Charles Fletcher, owner of the mill, built twenty-seven duplex houses on Pocasset and Maple Avenue in 1897–98, and added fourteen more on Walnut Street. The mill provided basic services and charged a nominal rent. The houses were sold in 1928.

This Ferri's Spa Soccer Team was the champion team for the 1928–29 season in the Rhode Island Junior Soccer League. Pictured, from left to right, are (front row) Fred Hudson, Pius Pansera, Carmine Labriole, Emile Fuoco, unknown, Tom Hanley, Fred Ferri, Carl Croce, and Anthony Scungio; (back row) Carl "Nation" (short for Combination) Simone, Jack Croce, Thomas Cabana, Anthony "Buffy" Ferri, unknown, and Andrew Ferri. (Photograph courtesy of Dorothy Ferri Willner.)

This very early view of soccer players from Thornton dates to c. 1890. On the left is Frank Smith; the boy is Winston Holyrod; and on the right is a German player, name unknown. A newspaper article states that soccer games played in Thornton in 1885 were some of the earliest, or the earliest, played in Rhode Island. In 1884, 120 English workers came over from Nottingham to work at the British Hosiery Mill. They provided the nucleus of Thornton's early soccer teams. (Photograph courtesy of Anthony Rainone.)

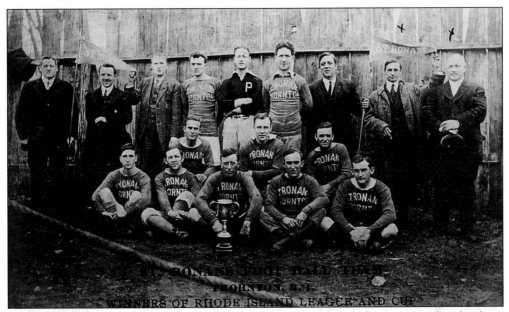

Saint Ronan's Soccer Team was sponsored by William Aitchison, who ran a hotel and cafe on Plainfield Street next to Ferri's Tap. He owned the land where Ferri's or Cricket Field is located and where his team played. The team broke up just before World War I. Aitchison was of Scottish background, so the team name probably came from the old country. (Photograph courtesy of Joe Coduri.)

The Vic's Boosters, a dedicated group of fans who supported Vic's Soccer Team (run by Butch Ferri), stand outside the old St. Rocco's Church. This scene from the 1930s shows Mary Ferri who ran the boosters (in front) and Jennie Rainone (in back of Mary). The boosters cheered at the Ferri Field games, sold tickets, and marched in parades in support of the team. (Photograph courtesy of Anthony Rainone.)

A view of the Johnston Theater in the early 1950s shows a lot of happy faces. Mario Votolato ran this theater on the second floor of the Ferri Block from about 1946 to the late 1960s. Mario's father, John, and later Mario operated a theater at Myrtle Hall from 1918 until 1942. The Ferri Block theater was run by Sid Richman and Bill Cappelli before Mario. (Photograph courtesy of Mario Votolato.)

The Swinghaven Canteen, started by Mario Votolato about 1946 in Myrtle Hall, was intended for older teens. Votolato later started the Junior Canteen for younger teens. This 1960 photograph shows the crowning of the king and queen at the Junior Canteen. Runner-up Susan Giansanti is crowning Lorraine Cardillo as queen, while Runner-up Pasco Macari is crowning Larry Caito as king. (Photograph courtesy of Mario Votolato.)

24

Pictured in 1930 is the Thornton Elementary School Drum Corps standing in front of the building. From left to right are Mario Votolato, Sandy LaFazia, Harold Goss, Domenic Cinami, Teddy Goss, Tommy Renzi, Ray Mendozzi, and Lillian Votolato. Note the drum with the cowboy on it. (Photograph courtesy of Mario Votolato.)

Young girls are shown marching in the 1942 St. Rocco's Parade. In the background is Benny Ricci's original gas station. The multi-day feast has been an important part of the village culture for most of this century. A statue of St. Rocco was carried from the old church on Clemence Street throughout the parade route each August 15th. There were parades for other saints in the parish, but St. Rocco's was always the biggest. (Photograph courtesy of Mario Votolato.)

The first St. Rocco's Church, shown in this *c.* 1915 postcard view, was built in 1903 on Clemence Street on the Cranston side of Thornton. From 1903 to 1907, it was a mission of the Holy Ghost Church in Providence. The rapidly growing Italian community of Thornton achieved parish status in 1907 and it has remained strong ever since. In 1951 the present St. Rocco's Church was built at 927 Atwood Avenue on the Johnston side.

Shown in this 1984 photograph, St. Brigid's Catholic Church is located at 1231 Plainfield Street. The church was built in 1914 and became a parish in 1915. Before this, missions from St. Ann's of Cranston and from St. Anthony's in Providence had served the English Catholic community of the village. The Reverend Edward J. O'Donnell was the first pastor.

The Holy Nativity Episcopal Church, shown in this c. 1915 postcard view, was built on Plainfield Street to serve the English immigrants who came over to work in the British Hosiery Mill. The rector of the Church of the Messiah in Olneyville was holding services in Thornton by 1887, possibly on the site of this building. The cornerstone of the present building was laid in 1900. No longer a church, it is used by the Knights of Columbus. (Photograph courtesy of Joe Coduri.)

This postcard scene, c. 1915, shows the Thornton Grammar School at 4 School Street. The size of the 1890 building reflects the expanding village population. Before that time, one- or two-room schools took care of the village needs. A 1919 fire burned the school to the ground. In 1921 the present brick school was completed.

The first junior high class at Thornton School was started in 1927. This 1942 graduating class shows four teachers in the front row from the second to the fifth positions: Miss Pascone, Miss Atwood, Vincent Rampone, and Nicky Ferri. In the middle row, first on right, is Mr. Waterman. (Photograph courtesy of Anthony Rainone.)

Benny Ricci is pictured in the late 1940s standing in front of his new gas station at the corner of Atwood Avenue and Plainfield Street. With him is John O. Pastore, Rhode Island's first Italian-American governor and senator. The station was built in the late 1940s before construction of the present St. Rocco's Church. (Photograph courtesy of Connie Ricci.)

Benny Ricci's service station is shown about 1950 or 1951. The new St. Rocco's Church is well along in construction on the left. This gas station replaced a smaller one on the site run by Mr. Ricci. The latter still stands at the Atwood Avenue curve in Cranston. The station pictured here was torn down in 1997 to make way for a drugstore. (Photograph courtesy of Connie Ricci.)

This late 1940s photograph shows, from left to right, John Don Francisco, Jimmy Goss, Henry Armstrong Sr., and Omer Laboissonniere. The men are in the basement of the Pocasset Worsted Mill, standing in front of a device designed by Armstrong to automatically feed textile machinery. These ball and creel devices were sold through his Armstrong Textile Co. Armstrong's son, Henry Jr., bought the Pocasset Mill from the Walter Marshall Spinning Co. (Photograph courtesy of Anna Armstrong.)

The Thornton Volunteers are seen with their 1923 Maxwell truck, the first in Thornton. Before this, two-wheeled hose carts were used. The driver is Duncan Turner and seated to his right is Chief Percy Brooks. Sitting on the hood is Albert Carrington and sitting on the running board is John Vanner. Standing on the truck are, from left to right, Pop Randall (?), ? Carrington, unknown , Mike Rossi, unknown, and Phillip Ricci. The identities of the three men standing on the ground are unknown. (Photograph courtesy of Anthony Rainone.)

In this April 1957 photograph are pictured the five vehicles of the Thornton Fire Station. On the left is Thornton's first ambulance, bought from North Providence. Second from the left is a 1948 Ford, a combination tanker and pumper. In the middle is a 1936 Maxim pumper, which is still at the station. Second from the right is 1957 (?) Seagrave pumper. On the far right is a 1941 Ford truck, converted to a brush fire vehicle by the volunteers. (Photograph courtesy of Mike Placella.)

Sitting atop the 1936 Maxim, Captain Mike Placella and the fire dog, Sparky, present a familiar view in 1957 at the Thornton Fire Station. Manned at that time by volunteers, the station is still owned by the Thornton Volunteer Fire Association. (Photograph courtesy of Mike Placella.)

Marching west in this 1950s parade, Thornton Fire Chief Ace Cappelli, in the white shirt on the right, leads the way. The parade is winding down Plainfield Street near Willow Street. On the right is Rosie's Snack Bar, a locally popular eating spot. The fireman in the tan uniform is Chief Wilfred Payette from the Lymansville Fire Station. (Photograph courtesy of Mike Placella.)

Pictured about 1957 are volunteer firemen from the Thornton firehouse who were fund-raising for the station. Left of the sign from left to right are Joe Russo and Roger Spina. Standing to the right of the sign are Anthony "Moo-Moo" Rossi and Jimmy Powers. Standing behind Moo-Moo on the truck are, from left to right, Harold "Chicky" Vanner, John Cappelli, and Angelo Cappelli Jr. Kneeling is Paul Melaragno. (Photograph courtesy of Mike Placella.)

Hiram Kimball Sr., the police chief, and Hiram Jr., his assistant, pose in front of town hall with the town's first police car, a 1934 RAO Flying Cloud. After the Olneyville/Silver Lake annexation to Providence in 1898, this building housed the police department, court, jail, and the town hall. The building still stands at 1343 Plainfield Street, but the town departments long ago moved elsewhere. (Photograph courtesy of Al Kimball.)

Two

Graniteville

Graniteville has been a thriving community for well over 150 years. Although it is often linked with the neighboring villages of Greystone and Centerdale in North Providence, it has always retained its identity. Textile mills in neighboring villages contributed to housing growth in Graniteville and, in turn, people from the latter sometimes shopped in Centerdale stores. Graniteville, though, had its own church, school, fire station, stores—such as Norris' Market and Chadwick's Corner Store—and even its own water system, using a windmill for power. For over ninety years a train line passed through the village, and a trolley line ran along Powder Mill Turnpike (now Route 44), which has long been a major link between Providence and points west. The turnpike name comes from a powder mill that was built in the village during the Revolutionary War, the only one ever built in Rhode Island.

The village name comes from the abundant granite deposits on Pine Hill. The Angell family owned much land here in the eighteenth and nineteenth centuries. Other early settlers were the Sweets, the Barnes's, and the Deans.

The Daniel Angell House, later the Olney W. Angell House, was the first home of the Angells in Graniteville. Situated on Dean Avenue, the west end of the house was built c. 1725, while the eastern portion was added prior to the Revolution. The Angells owned many hundreds of acres in Graniteville in the eighteenth and nineteenth centuries.

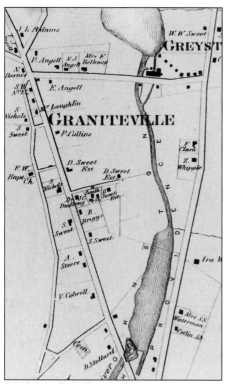

This 1870 map of Graniteville shows the village to be sparsely populated with about thirty houses spread out along Putnam Pike, Serrel Sweet Road, and Angell Avenue. The Baptist church is on Serrel Sweet Road with the original village school near the intersection with Putnam Pike. Five Sweet houses and three Angell houses can be seen. The Providence & Springfield Railroad is yet to be built.

The Farnum-Angell House, dating from 1825, was built by an unknown member of the Angell family as a two-family house. The second floor has exactly the same room arrangement as the first, including a bake oven in the keeping room. In 1870 it was the home of Prince Collins and was later owned by the Farnum family. Today, it is the home of the Johnston Historical Society. (Photograph courtesy of Kevin Neel.)

Built by the Sweet family and pictured in the 1930s, this house is located at 142 Putnam Pike. Willis Sweet, town official in the 1920s and 1930s, lived here. The Harrington family married into the Sweet family and later owned the house. Alex Harrington, who delivered milk for S.B. Winsor for many years, is the small boy on the left. (Photograph courtesy of Arthur Harrington.)

Harrington's Spa was located at 113 Putnam Avenue. George Harrington, the proprietor, was said to always have a cigar hanging out of his mouth. The spa was a popular hangout in the village, selling cigarettes, coffee, sandwiches, and ice cream. Next door to the spa was a First National Store. Today the building houses *The Community Press*. (Photograph courtesy of Arthur Harrington.)

George Harrington is pictured inside his spa, *c.* 1940. On the wall in back of him can be seen a wide variety of items from cigars, to tea, to a baseball glove. It is told that many neighborhood children learned to smoke here. (Photograph courtesy of Arthur Harrington.)

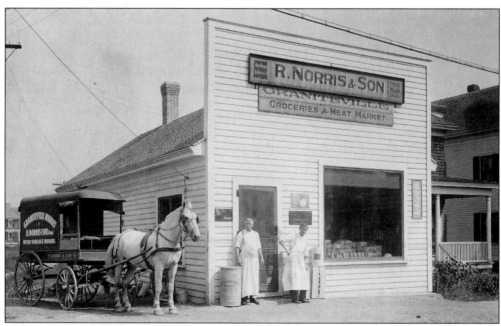

The Graniteville Market, R. Norris & Sons, Proprietors, was a popular variety store from the 1910s through the 1930s. It was located at 117 Putnam Avenue, at the corner of Cottage Avenue. Well-known for its meats and sausages, the side of the market's delivery wagon advertises the establishment as "noted sausage makers." (Photograph courtesy of Nellie Dahlin.)

The winter delivery vehicle of the Graniteville Market is shown here. The horse is wearing her winter attire and the sleigh carries bags of coal among other items. The driver, exposed to the elements, would probably have used a blanket too. (Photograph courtesy of Nellie Dahlin.)

Greystone Public Market

J. W. CHARNLEY, Prop.

Groceries, Meats and Provisions, Boots and Shoes, Dry Goods, Notions, Etc.

GRANITEVILLE, - - - - R. I.

Telephone Centredale 103-M

The Greystone Public Market was located at 22 Angell Avenue, off Putnam Avenue. The Charnley family ran the market from the 1910s into the 1930s and lived on the second floor. The building still stands but is now used for housing. (Photograph courtesy of Tom Greene.)

Mr. Chadwick stands outside his store in this scene from about 1910. Chadwick's Corner Store was situated at the corner of Angell Avenue and Putnam Pike. It is told that the first Gulf station in Rhode Island was located here. (Photograph courtesy of George Dansereau.)

Chadwick's Corner Store is viewed in the center of this *c.* 1920s photograph. The store was open from the early twentieth century to about 1964, at which time modern chain stores were killing off many old-time variety stores. A fairly large rock across Angell Avenue from the store was a favorite hangout for Graniteville youths for many years. (Photograph courtesy of George Dansereau.)

The house on the right in this *c.* 1920 view looking east down Putnam Avenue was owned by the Darby family. Alfred J. Darby was president of the Outlet Company in Providence, the largest department store in Rhode Island, from 1950 to 1960. The small building on the left was Poole's Shoe Shop. The photograph was taken from the yard of Reginald Thorpe, a well-known insurance agent in the village.

The white house in the center of this *c.* 1925 photograph belonged to Reverend Daniel Sweet, a minister at the nearby Graniteville church. About 1845 he built the large two-story barn to the right of this house. The barn was used to accommodate the local stagecoach, which ran from Pascoag to Providence. Horses were changed here for the second half of the trip. The structure was torn down *c.* 1970. (Photograph courtesy of Lora Clemence.)

Looking west into Johnston from the Centerdale Bridge, the first building seen on the left is the Foster & Gilson Tap. On the right is the train station of the New York, New Haven, and Hartford Railroad (formerly the Providence & Springfield Railroad). In back of the station the tall grain elevator can be seen in this 1913 photograph. (Photograph courtesy of RIDOT.)

Pictured about 1915 is the inside of the Foster & Gilson Tap on Putnam Pike across from the train station. The owner, Albert Foster, is behind the bar, waiting for customers ready to quench their thirst. In more modern times, the bar itself was removed and installed in the building next door, which operated as the Killarney Castle. The site is now a parking lot. (Photograph courtesy of Walter Foster.)

This turn-of-the-century photograph shows the 1859 Graniteville Baptist Church and the 1880 Graniteville School, both located on Serrel Sweet Road. The land for both structures was donated by Serrel Sweet. The school served the District #12 area until construction of the present school building in 1931. (Photograph courtesy of Robert Jackson.)

The Graniteville Baptist Church, shown here about 1920, was completed in 1859. Before this building was constructed, meetings were held in the homes of church members. The Elder Daniel A. Sweet was the congregation's leader during this period. The church traces its roots back to Elder Samuel Winsor's 1771 Six Principle Church in Belknap.

The interior of the 1880 Graniteville School is pictured here in 1925. It was the second school in the village, the first being a little further west on Serrel Sweet Road. The school was heated with wood-burning stoves and featured his and hers outhouses. (Photograph courtesy of Lora Clemence.)

The Graniteville Follies were held in the fire barn at the corner of Cottage and Putnam Avenues. Held in the 1920s and 1930s, the follies were run by Mrs. Harrington, who operated a local spa with her husband. The follies were performed on Friday and Saturday nights by local children. (Photograph courtesy of Arthur Harrington.)

The Graniteville School is located on Collins Avenue off Putnam Pike. It was erected in 1931 with major additions in 1968. This photograph from 1943 shows the graduating class. Herbie Brooks (in the second row on the left) was principal for many years. (Photograph courtesy of Arthur Harrington.)

Pictured here in September 1943 is the dedication of the Graniteville War Memorial. The serviceman on the right side of the white flag is Walter Pearson, a longtime Graniteville resident. The memorial services are still held each Memorial Day, when Graniteville residents show their strong patriotism, pride, and thankfulness for those who served their country.

The Graniteville Boy Scouts, Troop 1, met in the Graniteville church. Shown about 1963 are, from left to right, (front row) Raymond Baffoni, unknown, David Pincins, Jerry Porter, and Anthony Baffoni; (second row: leaders) Kenny Winchell, Arthur Jackson, and Mr. Snyder; (third row) Arthur Harrington, Gary Lynne, Stuart Pearson, Bobby Pincins, unknown, Bobby Scott, John Gregory, unknown, and John Van Orden; (fourth row) Joe Roukas, Ronnie Jackson, Joe Sousa, Glenn Scott, Jack Garnett, unknown, and unknown; (back row) Phillip Burgess, Donnie Seamens, unknown, David Scott, Dougie Gaunt, unknown, unknown, Robert Drake, and George Harrington. (Photograph courtesy of Arthur Harrington.)

The Graniteville Rovers, pictured here about 1933, were an amateur baseball team in the 1930s. They were sponsored by the Johnston GOP under Judge Stephen Siegel. The players shown are, from left to right, (front row) John Cafferty, Walt Whittingslow, Ray Yeager, Alfred Rushworth, Gill Charnley, Don Mumford, Denny Omerod, and Frances Cafferty; (back row) Tony Pezzulo, Fred Brown, Tom Lambie, Al Wood, Harold Nickelson, and Rolf Parr. (Photograph courtesy of Al Wood.)

The Graniteville Mohawks of the Johnston Little League are shown in 1957 at Cricket Field. Pictured are, from left to right, (front row) Mickey Beers, Ernie Parillo, unknown, Coach ?, Coach Alex Harrington, Manager Fred Brown, Bobby Scott, ? Mazilli, and Tommy Colardo; (back row) unknown, Scottie Moore, unknown, Butch Tracy, Terry Brown, and unknown. (Photograph courtesy of Alex Harrington.)

The Graniteville Volunteers' hook and ladder truck is pictured on Cottage Avenue during the 1920s. The truck was actually a Model A Ford automobile with a wagon attached to the back. The fireman in the white coat was Chief Fox. It was said that volunteers had to jump off and push the truck when there was a fire on Pine Hill. (Photograph courtesy of Donald Catley.)

Johnston's first ambulance, bought by the Graniteville volunteers in 1947, was a converted hearse. Pictured are, from left to right, Ken Aust, Harry Nelson, Eddie Simpson, unknown, Herbie Falls, and unknown. Before the station was remodeled as shown, the fire trucks entered it on the side of the building on the lower floor, and the first floor was used for things such as the Graniteville Follies. (Photograph courtesy of Vinnie Crosby.)

The Graniteville train station, captured here about 1920 and actually called the Centerdale Station, was built by the Providence & Springfield Railroad. The P&S provided both passenger and freight service until 1905 when the New Haven Railroad took over both roles. New Haven stopped carrying passengers in the 1930s and freight service ended in 1962. The station was torn down to make way for a Burger King. The grain elevator burned in the 1980s.

46

A busy restaurant in the village in the 1950s and 1960s, Lee's Cottage Restaurant was situated at 190 Putnam Pike. Legend has it that the building was built to look like a house in case the business failed. After the building burned to the ground, the point was moot.

The village of Graniteville is viewed from the Scout Field on what is now Steere Street. The Graniteville School is shadowed by the Worcester Textile Mill on the North Providence side. Many village residents worked in the mill under its present owners or back when it was run by the Joseph Benn Co. The Whitehall Building can be seen behind the mill. (Photograph courtesy of Ann Malone.)

The abundant granite outcroppings on Pine Hill were quarried for one hundred years. The Bear Rock Ledge Quarry (also spelled "Bare Rock") is shown here in 1997. The village takes its name from the rock on this hill, and evidence of the quarry's influence is seen all over the village in the walls, foundations, and steps that are built from cut granite. Emor Angell, Harry Carey, and Albert Lippett were quarrymen who worked the hill.

The granite columns for the 1822 Arcade in Providence, pictured here, were taken from the Bear Rock Ledge Quarry on Pine Hill in Graniteville. Said to be the second largest granite monoliths in the country, the columns were hauled to Providence by James Olney using teams of oxen.

Three
Hughesdale

Hughesdale is a small, quiet village, although at one point in the nineteenth century it was bustling with activity. At that time, there were three textile mills operating within a few hundred yards of each other along Dry Brook, which flows through the village and feeds into the Pocasset River. James F. Simmons, Thomas and Theodore Hughes, and Zenas Bliss were some of the major figures involved here in the production of textiles or textile soap and chemicals from the 1830s to the early twentieth century. A local flood in 1868 wiped out the three mill dams and most of the manufacturing complexes in the village. The upper and lower sites were rebuilt, once again turning out textiles and textile soap. Bradford Soap Works was situated at the lower site for a number of years. A 1914 fire stopped industrial activity here, although an icehouse continued to operate at the upper pond.

Until the 1930s Hughesdale had a church, a school, and a store. Worker housing was provided, including at least two stone duplexes. Farms and dairies in the area included ones run by the Mathewson, Wilder, Walch, and Toby families.

Much of the village of Hughesdale shown on this 1870 map remains intact; the school, the store, the owner's house, some workers' housing, and the upper and lower dams are still in place. The mills and the church are now gone.

Thomas Hughes, one of the early mill owners here, built this modest but handsome Greek Revival dwelling in the heart of the village at 423 Central Avenue. In later times with corporations owning the mills, owners would seek out more fashionable addresses in Providence. Hughes started the Hughesdale Dye & Chemical Works and the Glendale Chemical Works and ran them until his death in 1884.

A stone mill house formerly belonging to the Hughesdale Chemical Works is pictured here. Built of fieldstone in the early nineteenth century with very thick walls, two of these houses remain along Central Avenue. Pictured in the 1980s, this one stands pretty much unchanged, while the one to its west has been covered with modern siding.

These unusual artifacts from the nineteenth century are reminders of the early textile soap and chemical industry that operated at the lower mill site. It is thought that chemicals were mixed in these granite vats. There are about seven of them, most of them long and deep, resembling watering troughs. Steve Merolla stands alongside a square vat with a bowl-shaped depression in 1997.

Theodore Hughes, son of Thomas Hughes, took over the manufacturing of textile chemicals after his father died in 1884. Pictured here in 1908, Hughes managed the company until a fire destroyed the complex in 1914. He also served in the state legislature for five years. His home still stands on Central Avenue, just west of his father's house. It has been greatly altered.

In the early twentieth century, Judge Andrew Patton lived in this home on the south side of Central Avenue, pictured here in 1984. His ancestor, James Patton, was an engraver and resided here in 1870. The family lived here from at least 1851 to the middle of the twentieth century, when the house passed out of family. In 1917 the Patton property took up the whole southwest corner of Atwood and Central Avenues, totaling 10 acres.

In 1870 this house on Atwood Avenue was owned by a J. Smith family. Dating from the early nineteenth century and pictured here in 1975, it lasted until the 1980s when it was torn down. (Photograph courtesy of Walter Nebiker, RIHP&HC.)

This 1927 photograph was taken by the state to show the bridge on Atwood Avenue over Dry Brook, which feeds into the Pocasset River. Looking north the Hughesdale store is seen, probably on its original site. The Thornton/Hughesdale trolley line terminated just out of view. (Photograph courtesy of RIDOT.)

Moved back slightly from the modern road, this original village store now functions as a convenience store for a gas station at the intersection of Central and Atwood Avenues. The building, here by 1870, was photographed in 1997. It also served as the village post office from 1876 to 1916 with Theodore S. Hughes serving as postmaster.

This 1928 photograph shows construction at the Hughesdale Bridge, which spans Dry Brook at Atwood Avenue. Since this was a state bridge, the men pictured would be state workers or workers on a construction crew hired by the state. (Photograph courtesy of RIDOT.)

Damaged beyond repair by the 1938 hurricane, the Hughesdale church was the only one in the three neighboring villages of Morgan Mills, Hughesdale, and Simmonsville. In 1870 it was listed as the Union Church. Later it was a Congregational church and finally a Methodist-Episcopal church. It stood on the northeast corner of the Atwood Avenue-Central Avenue intersection. (Photograph courtesy of Mabel Sprague.)

Looking west along Central Pike in this c. 1910 postcard view, the Hughesdale School is seen on the right. The next two buildings were owned by the Hughes family, the far one being Thomas Hughes' house.

The Hughesdale School was a typical country school. In use by 1862, it is still standing on Central Avenue and now houses a nursery. This 1984 photograph shows that the building's cupola has been removed. This was the school for the Dry Brook District #13.

This c. 1885 photograph looks east along Central Avenue, with the Judge Patton House on the right. The village store is in the distance also on the right side. On the left is the Thomas Hughes House at 423 Central Avenue. The Miller family lived here after the Hughes family. Charles Miller was a chauffeur for the Hugheses. The second house from the left is 417 Central Avenue and was also owned by the Hughes family. (Photograph courtesy of Mabel Sprague.)

This c. 1885 photograph looks west towards Hughesdale following the line of Central Avenue from the Wilder property. On the extreme right is Bill Kent's house. He was a high sheriff around the turn of the century. Charlie Brown later bought the property. Next is the Hughesdale church and left of the church is James Patton's house. Then comes the school, part of it blocked from view by the store. (Photograph courtesy of Mabel Sprague.)

Four
Morgan Mills

Long a sleepy, isolated hamlet, much of Morgan Mills has been divided into house lots in recent years. The village grew up around an early textile mill built about 1817 along the Pocasset River near Morgan Avenue. A number of houses predate the mill, though, and Morgan Avenue was already in existence as part of the old Scituate Road.

There was a village store, but no church or school was ever built here, residents having to use facilities at neighboring villages. Local farms or dairies included those worked by the Alversons, the Tillinghasts, the Crandalls, the Atwoods, the Wilders, the Harrises, and the Onsleys. The farms have closed, the mill is gone, and only the old farmhouses remain to show this was once a village.

On the Alverson farm in the twentieth century, owner Colonel Frank W. Tilinghast let the local Native Americans hold pow-wows on his land. There were Native Americans still living in the village at this time, and Indian Rock (or Hipse's Rock), an important landmark, is located just south of his farm.

The name Morgan comes from the Sprague family, who owned the mill in the mid-nineteenth century. Amasa Sprague's father-in-law was named Young Morgan. Leander W. Peckham purchased the mill in 1896.

Morgan Mills, shown on this 1870 map, depended on neighboring villages for schools and churches. With the loss of its mill and with the development of new housing plats, it has lost much of its village identity. Morgan Avenue runs through the center of the village.

Built around 1789 by Abraham C. Atwood, this house has grown in size with many additions. The original house is the tallest section shown. Still lived in by Atwood's great-granddaughter, Mabel (Atwood) Sprague, the house stands at 216 Morgan Avenue. (Photograph courtesy of Mabel Sprague.)

An early view, c. 1880s, shows two major farms in the village, the Abraham Atwood farm in the foreground and the Welcome Alverson farm in the distance, on the north side of Morgan Avenue. All the outbuildings in the right foreground burned in 1910. To the left of the big barn is the original Alverson House, still standing but with many changes. (Photograph courtesy of Mabel Sprague.)

Hiram Atwood built this house at 281 Morgan Avenue around 1845 on 10 acres he purchased from Samuel Randall. He is said to have finished rooms inside only as they were needed—he and his two wives had eleven children. In 1875 he sold the house to James Lincoln and moved across the street to his father's farm. Lincoln later sold the property to Joseph Webb and it was passed on to his grandson, Webb Wilder. (Photograph courtesy of Harold Beaudoin.)

The house on the left at 285 Morgan Avenue was built by Joseph Webb about 1885 or 1890 after he bought the Hiram Atwood House on the right at number 281. Webb lived in the Atwood House and rented out this house (number 285, also known as the Evans house). The two houses look much the same today. (Photograph courtesy of Harold Beaudoin.)

Members of the D'Acchioli family are seen on their farm in the 1920s. Their farm was located on Atwood Avenue just opposite Old Scituate Avenue. In the middle is Cosmo D'Acchioli Sr. On the left is his sister, Madeline, and on the right is their nephew, Tom Marandola. They are harvesting a type of dandelion-like green. The D'Acchiolis were also known for the anise they grew. In the background can be seen the Webb Wilder and Evans homesteads on Morgan Avenue. (Photograph courtesy of D'Acchioli family.)

Built about 1817 by Christopher Harris and Christopher Atwood, the textile mill in Morgan Mills lasted until the 1970s when it burned to the ground. The trapdoor monitor, an early feature, provided light for the upper story. Located just to the south of Morgan Avenue, it used the Pocasset River for power. Samson Almy ran the mill in the 1820s, followed by a Mathewson, William Larcher, the Spragues, the Pierces, and Leander W. Peckham in 1896. (Photograph courtesy of Rich LaFazia.)

Operated by Joseph Webb, this small store served the Morgan Mills village during the early twentieth century. Located on Morgan Avenue just to the east of number 276, the building was torn down in the early 1930s. Webb lived across the street at 281 Morgan Avenue before his death about 1925. Two others tried with little success to run the store, an Edward Radigan and a John Shaw. (Photograph courtesy of Earl Blamires.)

The Welcome Alverson Homestead, pictured about 1890, is viewed from the Abraham Atwood property. The main house, a Greek Revival style structure from the 1830s or 1840s, stands today but with a porch across the front, dormers, and a large ell on the rear. The small houses to the right are said to have been slave houses. They are now gone. The ell on the back of the house in this view was the kitchen.

Othello Godfrey, a Civil War veteran, lived in the early twentieth century in a wood frame building on the old path to the mill. Remembered as a kindly man, he was well liked by the neighborhood children. He would allow his horse to come inside the doorway to his house to be fed tidbits. On major holidays he would fire off his gun in celebration. (Photograph courtesy of Mabel Sprague.)

Leander W. Peckham, third from the right, and his wife, Josephine Bennett, second from the right, are pictured in this c. 1900 scene. The other two women are thought to be her sisters. Enjoying their day on the water, the Peckhams were leading the good life, facilitated by their successful textile business. Their home at 278 Morgan Avenue was said by locals to have been built for show. It is standing but has been severely altered. (Photograph courtesy of Mabel Sprague.)

Of much area importance, this rock was a marker for Roger Williams' original land purchase from the Narragansett Indian chiefs in 1638. Still in place, the rock, known as Hipses Rock, is located west of Vincent Drive off Morgan Avenue. The three adults in the center of this *c.* 1890 photograph are Edmund Atwood (left), Waldo Cranston (center), and Waldo's sister (right). (Photograph courtesy of Mabel Sprague.)

This late-nineteenth-century view shows a gold mine in back of the 1025 Banquet Hall on Plainfield Street. Mabel Sprague's father remembers a shaft being worked about 1875. He thought that it was sugared. (Photograph courtesy of Mabel Sprague.)

Lorenzo (Larry) Coletti appears in his barbershop at 1184 Atwood Avenue. Pictured here about 1920, Larry's Barbershop was on the first floor of a three-story tenement. Adjoining the shop was a poolroom. About 1925 he converted a garage on the property into a new barbershop. He died in 1981, aged ninety-two years, having run his shop until he was ninety. (Photograph courtesy of Anna Coletti Armstrong.)

This 1939 calendar illustration shows the E.S. Crandall Dairy on Morgan Avenue. The building on the left is the Welcome Alverson House, in the Greek Revival style. Colonel Frank W. Tillinghast bought the farm in 1898 and sold cows and milk. In 1938 the Crandall Dairy moved from Providence into their new barn pictured here. Their help, all dressed in white, took care of sixty Guernsey cows. The house and barn still stand. (Photograph courtesy of Mabel Sprague.)

E. S. CRANDALL DAIRY

Milk and Cream • Grade "A" Guernsey Milk

Fresh Daily From Our Own R. I. Herd. Sealed in Cellophane for Your Protection.

WEst 4358   **PROVIDENCE**   **12 Lowell Ave.**

Five

Manton

Straddling the Providence-Johnston border, Manton village is centered on the intersection of the old Killingly Road (the present Greenville Avenue) and the Woonasquatucket River. Early houses in the area indicate that settlement goes back to the mid- or late seventeenth century, making Manton one of the first areas in the town to be populated. The Manton & Kelley Mill, just on the Providence side, was built in the 1820s and was an impetus to growth of the village. By 1835 the village was called Tripptown, named after an early family in the area. In the 1840s it was called Rockville and in 1849 the Manton name came into use when a post office was established here.

A train line and later a trolley line passed through the village, carrying goods and people to and from Providence and points west. A limestone quarry and kiln located west of Killingly Street, so important for building houses, may have been one of the first in Rhode Island. Schools and churches were present by the mid-nineteenth century. Some prominent local families were the Smiths, the Clemences, the Mantons, the Tripps, the Whites, and the Barneses.

Manton village, shown here in 1870, is divided between Providence and Johnston on the left; the Woonasquatucket River is the dividing line. The main road running left to right is Manton Avenue on the Providence side and Greenville Avenue on the Johnston side of the river.

Shown in this 1891 view, the Clemence/Irons House is located on George Waterman Road. It is sometimes mistakenly referred to as the Edward Manton House. Besides the Clemences, other occupants of the house were the Angells, the Goddards, the Sweets, and the Ironses. After Nellie Irons died in 1937, Henry D. Sharpe bought the house and commissioned its restoration. (Photograph courtesy of Gina Perrotta.)

The Clemence/Irons House, shown in this modern photograph, was built around 1680 by Thomas Clemence or his son, Richard. It is now owned by the Society for the Preservation of New England Antiquities. This "Rhode Island stone-ender" was restored in 1939 and 1940 by Thomas Isham. The huge stone-end chimney was built of local stone with mortar probably made from lime from the nearby limestone quarry in Manton. (Photograph courtesy of Mohr Library.)

This page from a 1910 Johnston Directory shows the Manton Hotel on Greenville Avenue not far from the Providence line. Situated on the old Killingly Road, the hotel was operating by 1852 but the building itself dates to the eighteenth century. After its days as a hotel ended, it was used as a cafe until it was torn down about 1984.

MANTON HOTEL

MANTON, R. I.

F. H. LEONARD, Proprietor

Automobile Parties Accommodated

Clerk, PETE CLARK   Telephone West 9197

The Barnes family homestead, shown in 1976, was torn down soon after this photograph was taken. Located on Greenville Avenue near Cherry Hill Road, it was for many years the home of Sarah Dyer Barnes, a longtime teacher in Providence and Johnston, an activist in political and educational affairs, and one of the first female school superintendents in Rhode Island. The local school is named after her. (Photograph courtesy of Walter Nebiker, RIHP&HC.)

Owned in 1870 by Jonathan S. Kelley, owner of the Manton Mill, the Leroy White House was later purchased by George White. George's son, Leroy White Sr., and later his grandson, Leroy Jr., ran a successful farm here at the northwest corner of Cherry Hill Road and Greenville Avenue. The simply adorned homestead was torn down about 1990 after Leroy Jr. died.

Edward J. Mathewson is shown working on the Leroy White farm. Mathewson was the stepson of Clarabel (White) Mathewson, the daughter of George White. (Photograph courtesy of Whytebrook Terrace.)

Torn down around 1990, this huge barn was the focal point of the Leroy White farm. Leroy White is shown taking the horses out for a day's work. (Photograph courtesy of Whytebrook Terrace.)

Leroy White Jr. poses with a young calf in 1958 at the Leroy White farm. The Whites kept cows and sold milk from the barn, 5¢ a pint and 10¢ a quart. They also grew sugar and corn. (Photograph courtesy of Whytebrook Terrace.)

In a sad moment for many local residents, around 1990 the Leroy White Barn was torn down. Deemed unsafe, it was quickly brought to the ground. The barn was also a victim of the times. What do you do with a big old barn now that dairying is a thing of the past in the town?

Joseph and Rosa (Stark) Newman are seen about 1890 with their five children, Fred, Arthur, Walter, Otto, and Eddie. Joseph came over from Germany, built the family farm at Bucklin and Greenville Avenues, and in 1879 started the Newman Dairy. His offspring continued running the dairy under various names for many years. (Photograph courtesy of Herb Newman.)

Haying about 1913 on the Newman Farm off Greenville Avenue is Otto Newman with his son Wilton. The house on the right is on Osgood Avenue. Otto never ran the farm. (Photograph courtesy of Herb Newman.)

Walter Newman is the driver of the delivery wagon for the Newman Brothers' Dairy. Clint Nickerson, a neighborhood boy, stands with him. Walter and Arthur Newman, sons of Joseph Newman, ran the dairy together in the early twentieth century. At some point they were running dairies separately under the names A.J. Newman and W.C. Newman. (Photograph courtesy of Herb Newman.)

This 1930 photograph shows the Prophet Spring Water Co. at the corner of Greenville Avenue and Spring Hill Avenue. William MacMillan ran the business. (Photograph courtesy of MacMillan family.)

This c. 1935 photograph shows a parade put on by Manton Hose Co. #3 heading east on Greenville Avenue. The two-story building in the center housed the First National Store, and the Manton Baptist Church shows in the distance. The members of the group in the center are either sea scouts or sea cadets.

Another view of the same parade shows the Joseph Newman House on the right at the corner of Bucklin Avenue. The policeman in front is Tom Kennedy and the World War I veteran to his left is Emilio Ferranti. The three Hose Co. #3 fireman (in white shirts) are, from left to right, Charlie Quinn, George McElroy, and Paul Jacques.

This *c.* 1912 photograph shows students of the Lincoln School, located on Greenville Avenue just west of where George Waterman Avenue begins. The building is now gone. (Photograph courtesy of Herb Newman.)

The Manton School is shown in the early twentieth century on Greenville Avenue just west of Killingly Street. Its large size shows how much the village had grown. In the 1970s the building housed the town school administration offices. It was demolished after that.

The George C. Calef School is seen when it was new. Located on Waveland Avenue off Killingly Street, the school was only one year old when this 1924 photograph was taken. Calef, a Vermont native, came to this area as a young man and became a successful businessman. He was very active in the Manton School District and on the town school committee. (Photograph courtesy of Lora Clemence.)

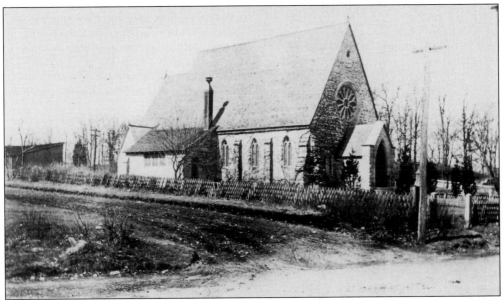

St. Peter's, an English-style, stone church was built in 1855 on the northern end of Killingly Street from plans by noted Rhode Island architect Thomas Tefft. Pictured here about 1915, it replaced an earlier wood-frame structure built in 1846 and still standing across the street. The stone church burned in 1972, but the congregation joined with St. Andrew's in Providence and still exists.

The Manton Baptist Church was dedicated in 1889 but continued as a missionary effort of the Central Baptist Church in Providence until 1913. At that time it became a full-fledged parish. By the late 1930s it had stopped functioning as a church and the building burned to the ground in recent years.

Francesco DelVecchio and his wife, Maria Guesepina (Carfagnina) DelVecchio, are shown at home on Lafayette Street. They arrived in Johnston in the 1890s. Their youngest child, Clara Mills, lives at their home. DelVecchio was a founding member of the Della Difesa Society, formed in the 1900s by immigrants from Casa Calenda, Italy, who settled in Manton. DelVecchio was a constable and an influential man in the village. He was nicknamed the "mayor" because of the assistance he offered the immigrants. (Photograph courtesy of Clara Mills.)

Mary Casale, age three in this 1931 picture, is wearing an angel costume brought over from Italy. She was the traditional angel of the procession at the 1931 Feast of the Madonna Della Difesa at Our Lady of Grace Church. She was strapped into a harness and hoisted over the statue of the Virgin Mary to be carried along in the parade. Mary said she was terrified. (Photograph courtesy of Mary Casale Carroll.)

A crowd is enjoying the Feast of Madonna Della Difesa in the late 1940s. This annual feast at Our Lady of Grace Church continues to play an important role in the Italian community. The parish was formed in 1912 and for many years held one of the largest festivals of Italian heritage in the local area. The feast attracted people from as far away as Canada. It continues today on a smaller scale. (Photograph courtesy of Eileen Perriello.)

This 1940s view of Our Lady of Grace Church was taken during the Feast of the Madonna Della Difesa. To serve the religious needs of the Catholics in Manton a mission was formed in the 1910s. The mission grew and soon the parish of Our Lady of Grace was formed. The photograph shows two bandstands, allowing continuous entertainment. Two of the bands that played here were the Natick Band from the Italian community in West Warwick and the Ferri Band from Thornton. (Photograph courtesy of Eileen Perriello.)

The Hep Cat Canteen, held upstairs in the hall at the Manton Fire Station, is shown in the late 1940s or early 1950s. Mario Votolato, seen on drums in the rear, started the canteen at the request of Mrs. Barrett, who then took over and ran the canteen and a youth center for a number of years. (Photograph courtesy of Mario Votolato.)

The Manton train station, pictured here about 1920, was on the Providence & Springfield Railroad line. Once passengers and freight were carried on this route, but the New Haven Railroad terminated passenger services in the 1930s, carrying only freight after that. In 1962 the last train traveled the line. In the nineteenth century this station was occasionally used for church services. (Photograph courtesy of Fred Corcoran.)

The Manton Hose Co. #3 is in front of the old Manton fire barn. This photograph was probably taken at the turn of the century. A proud, well-disciplined crew, the Manton volunteers selflessly answered the call to save property and lives. The hose co. was organized on April 7, 1892, under William H. King, foreman. (Photograph courtesy of Manton Hose Co. #3.)

This c. 1900 view shows the Manton Hose Company #3 with its fire wagon on Greenville Avenue just south of Cherry Hill Road. From left to right are William King (foreman), Asa Hicks, George Miner, Dan Farrell, Charles Billings, Charles Bates, Hiram King, George Barnes (second assistant foreman), John Coughlin (hose cart driver), Charles Adams (councilman, near the porch), George Harril, Frank Flannigan, Ira Evans, Gus Dadrick, and Ed Powell.

The station was built in 1913 by the Manton Hose Co. #3. It is still standing and still owned by the volunteers, but it is no longer used as a firehouse. Standing in front of the 1924 Seagrave pumper are, from left to right, Frank Volley, Frank Hanfield, Robert Frazer, Henry Gandett, Oscar Bouchard, Everett Smith, Sam Black, Thomas Kennedy, and A. Robert Black. The driver is Allen Smith (Photograph courtesy of Manton Hose Co. #3.)

This vehicle was converted by the volunteers for use as a fire-fighting wagon. In this 1940s photograph are, from left to right, unknown, ? Torrelli (?), Joe Scott, Bill Jasper, ? Ferrante, unknown, Harvey Shaw, unknown, Stephen Tassa, "Tukey" McCoy, and Charles Quinn. (Photograph courtesy of Manton Hose Co. #3.)

Six
Simmonsville

Simmonsville, quiet today, was a bustling village in the nineteenth century. James Fowler Simmons started the textile industry here after he purchased a stone building in 1822 for that purpose from his father-in-law, Judge Samuel Randall. The Randall family was one of the first to settle in the village, and their house still stands. Simmons' mill was situated along Cedar Swamp Brook, which provided a good source of waterpower. Other textile men followed him, including Reuben Mathewson, William A. Pirce, and Benjamin Almy. A disastrous flood caused by a dam break in 1840 took eighteen lives in the village. Two larger and much sturdier holding reservoirs, Simmons Upper and Lower Reservoirs, were built in mid-century to provide a steady flow of water to the mills.

The mills were not large ones, though, and Simmonsville never attained the importance of its sister village, Thornton. By the early twentieth century much of the land here was abandoned by the early English settlers and had been bought by Italian-Americans who engaged in the truck vegetable trade, flower growing, and cider production. Some of the early Italian families were the Gattas, the Russos, the Tartaglias, and the Ucifferos.

The Randall family, one of the first in the area, lived at this house at 132 Simmonsville Avenue. The house dates to the eighteenth century. Judge Samuel Randall ran a gristmill and a textile mill here in the early nineteenth century. The Russo family has lived in the house for many years.

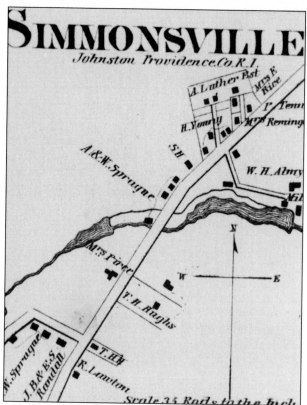

Simmonsville, or Simmons Upper Village, is centered on Simmonsville Avenue where it passes over Cedar Swamp Brook. Settlement goes back to at least the eighteenth century as evidenced by the Randall House, seen here on this 1870 map. James F. Simmons was operating a textile mill here in 1822.

Benjamin Pirce, a local textile manufacturer, lived in this house at 150 Simmonsville Avenue. William, son of Benjamin, was Johnston's only U.S. representative. For many years the house has been owned by the Ruotolo family who ran the Old Mill Dairy, named for the old textile mill ruin that stood on their property (see next illustration).

This drawing from an 1890 newspaper shows the Old Mill, now long gone. Once located on Simmonsville Avenue where it is crossed by Cedar Swamp Brook, the mill structure lasted well into this century. No trace remains today. The buildings to the right of the mill were stone mill houses. None of the three houses remain.

This ruin, showing finely crafted stone construction, was once a textile mill run by the Almy family. It sits on the south side of Almy Street, opposite the stone mill house. An unused water wheel was said to been present in the early part of this century.

Stone worker houses are relatively rare in Rhode Island, but were built in four Johnston villages: Simmonsville, Hughesdale, Thornton, and Morgan Mills. This house, photographed in 1975, lasted on Simmonsville Avenue until the 1980s. It is portrayed in the 1890 drawing on page 83. (Photograph by Walter Nebiker, RIHP&HC.)

At least seven of these stone rubble mill houses were erected in the village in the early nineteenth century. Of the three remaining, only one, at the end of Almy Street, retains its original exterior finish. The Russo family lived here in the early twentieth century and Johnston's first mayor, Ralph Russo, was born here. It was torn down in the 1980s. (Photograph by Walter Nebiker, RIHP&HC.)

Son of a textile manufacturer in the village, Zenas Bliss was born in Simmonsville in 1835. He entered West Point at age fifteen and graduated in 1854. During the Civil War he performed actions that later won him a Congressional Medal of Honor. Staying in the army, he went on to command many posts on the frontier during his forty-seven-year career as an officer (which is believed to be a record). He rose to the rank of major general and is buried in Washington, D.C. (Photograph courtesy of Zenas W. Bliss II.)

Hiram Kimball, chief of police in Johnston from 1898 to 1934, was also holder of many other positions in town such as overseer of the poor, health officer, and dog officer. Since Kimball was a very young man when this picture was taken, it is estimated to be c. 1890. He lived on Simmonsville Avenue at the corner of Kimball Avenue until his death in 1938. (Photograph courtesy of Joseph Russo.)

Serving the village in the early twentieth century, the building on the left is a store that dates back to at least the early 1930s. In the 1940s and 1950s it was run by "Carmooch" Scungio. The man in the convertible is John Colizzo. (Photograph courtesy of Joe Uciferro.)

This 1948 state photograph, looking north, shows work in progress on Simmonsville Avenue. On the right an old mill pond has been drained. In the distance on the right is a large stone worker house. The second building on the left was Scungio's Store and two doors down was another store. (Photograph courtesy of RIDOT.)

This photograph was taken one month after the previous shot and shows the new retaining wall on the east side of Simmonsville Avenue. The second building on the right is the 1850s school, long-forgotten but still standing today. The second building from the left is one of the stone mill houses that are now gone. (Photograph courtesy of RIDOT.)

Aaron DeMoranville, Johnston superintendent of schools, was asked by the state during World War II to locate farms that had images worthy of photographic preservation. Photographed on the Russo farm at 132 Simmonsville Avenue are, from left to right, Vincent Russo, Ida (Russo) Acciardo, and Madeline (Russo) Travellini. Their patches show the letters VFV (Vegetables for Victory) and FFF (Food for Freedom). (Photograph courtesy of Russo family.)

The third and final Simmonsville school is pictured here in 1933 or 1934 on Kimball Avenue. Pictured from left to right are (front row) M. Testa, V. Fradon, E. Morro, M. Russo, J. Carnavale, B. Melone, A. Maranadola, F. Russo, I. Russo, L. Macera, and M. Ricci; (middle row) T. Uciferro, J. Colizzo, F. Delellis, A. Russo, G. Colizzo, A. DelFino, A. Russo, J. Cafaro, C. Russo, G. Melone, L. Altrui, J. Morra, and C. Russo; (back row) L. Marandola, T. Rossi, J. Rossi, J. Landi, J. Gatta, A. Ferrante, J. Stralewski, M. Scungio, R. DelFino, and V. DiDonato. (Photograph courtesy of DelFino family.)

This village school on Kimball Avenue was built in 1916 and operated into the 1950s. There were two rooms, one for grades one through three and the other for grades four through six. In the early 1920s, a Ruth Lindahl taught the early grades and Jennie De Fusco taught the older children. (Photograph courtesy of Ann Parrillo.)

Seven
Pocasset

Pocasset, not a place name found on a map, has been a vital area of the town for most of the past 150 years. Its central location on the Hartford Road where it is crossed by the Pocasset River, the Pocasset Road, and Atwood Avenue made it a place of importance by the early nineteenth century. Following the Dorr War and our initial state constitution, Johnston in the 1840s built its first town house in the village on the north side of the Hartford Road, near the present Johnston Memorial Park. By mid-century, a bleachery, a wheelwright shop, and a blacksmith shop were clustered along the river nearby.

As the nineteenth century rolled along, Olneyville and Thornton became the dominant villages in town, sharing the town offices from the 1870s to the 1930s. At that time, town officials once again realized the importance of Pocasset's central location. In the 1930s they built the new town hall and police station at the intersection of Hartford and Atwood Avenues. In the 1960s and 1970s, the high school (now Ferri Middle School), the Mohr Library, the fire department headquarters, the new high school, and finally the new police station were added.

The Thornton House, built in the eighteenth century, stood on Memorial Drive at Atwood Avenue. Long occupied by the Thornton family and last lived in by the LaFazia family, the house was dismantled and re-erected about 1990 in Ohio. (Photograph by Walter Nebiker, RIHP&HC.)

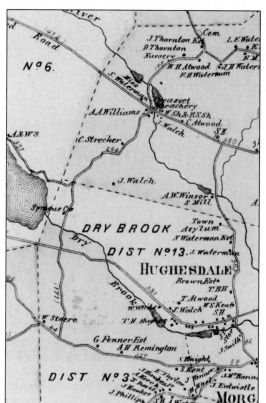

This 1870 map shows how lightly developed Pocasset was at that time. The village encompassed the upper third of the map. The Hartford Road runs east and west and the old Pocasset Road runs north and south. One hundred years later this section was booming and today it continues to grow.

An eighteenth-century farm building belonging to the Waterman family, this house played an interesting part in the Revolution. Afraid that the British would sail up the bay and occupy Providence, the latter's town fathers in 1777 moved the town records to this house for safekeeping. In 1779 they were returned; the Waterman House, way out in the wilderness, had helped the war effort in its own small way. Torn down in the 1960s, the building previously stood at the end of Cherry Hill Road at Atwood Avenue. (Photograph courtesy of Irving Almonte.)

John Nanni of the Johnston Historical Society examines the center chimney of the Thornton House during its dismantling in the 1980s. Possessing many fine early features such as period mantles and a finished food storage room in the basement, the house was re-erected and beautifully restored in Greenville, Ohio.

Built in the 1840s following the Dorr War and Rhode Island's initial constitution, this first town house served the town for about thirty years until offices were located in the more built-up Olneyville area. Photographed in 1975, the building was torn down about 1990. (Photograph by Walter Nebiker, RIHP&HC.)

Looking west along the Hartford Pike, this 1928 view shows the Pocasset River Bridge. A Socony gas station with one pump is on the left. The greenhouse next to it is part of the Alfred A. Williams property. Austin's Plantarama later used a portion of that estate. (Photograph courtesy of RIDOT.)

One of two "portable" schools in town, Pocasset School, pictured here in 1925, was a wood frame building resting on cinder block legs. At that time it served the children of District 5, which was centered on the Hartford Pike at Atwood Avenue. It is long gone. (Photograph courtesy of Lora Clemence.)

This interior view of the Pocasset portable school, one of up to sixteen district schools in the town, was taken in 1925. Another portable school, a twin of this one, was on Brown Avenue. (Photograph courtesy of Lora Clemence.)

Built during the Depression from designs by Oresto DiSaia, Johnston's second town hall additionally housed the police department and the jail until 1966. From 1870 until 1933, the town rented space for the town offices. This town hall opened for business in 1933 and has housed the offices of town government ever since.

Albert Ferruolo, a past Johnston building inspector, was a champion motor-paced bicycle racer. In 1933 he was the winner of the Eastern Motor Pace Championship at the Providence Cycledrome on North Main Street. His brother, Jimmy, was an excellent motor-pacer who traveled all over the U.S. with his motorcycle. Albert lived most of his adult life off Hartford Avenue in Johnston. (Photograph courtesy of Phyllis Ferruolo.)

One of the oldest operating gas stations in town, Mancini's service station is pictured here in the early 1940s. It was started by John Mancini, who still works at the station. Today it is a Getty station, located at 1191 Hartford Avenue. (Photograph courtesy of John Mancini.)

Dedicated in 1945, Johnston Memorial Park on Hartford Avenue was constructed as a memorial to the town's men and women who served their country during World War II. Private citizens, businesses, and groups donated a wide variety of items such as trees, fireplaces, flagpoles, wiring, etc.

DEDICATED TO OUR
WORLD WAR II VETERANS

MEMORIAL DAY
NINETEEN HUNDRED and FORTY-SIX

The Velvet Inn on Hartford Avenue featured "Italian Cooking and American food" (maybe the latter was not cooked?) for their stop-and-go patrons and "heated cabins" for the over-nighters. The inn was located on Hartford Avenue a short distance west of Pocasset Road.

A local landmark for many years, the Ranch House was located at 1460 Hartford Avenue, just west of Atwood Avenue. Built after World War II, it could hold one thousand people. Described as an elegant supper club, it hosted big-time performers such as Patti Page. It was gone by the early 1960s.

In 1959 Johnston celebrated the 200th anniversary of its independence from Providence. A large parade with numerous floats highlighted the festivities. This decorated truck was prepared by Mancini's service station on Hartford Avenue. (Photograph courtesy of John Mancini.)

Eight
The West End

The area of town known today as the West End has never been an official village or region. It is basically the area west of Route 295 that runs north and south to the town line. Never highly developed, this western half of Johnston showed little industrial or commercial activity for most of the history of the town. The Johnston map from the 1870 *Beers Atlas* shows no churches or textile mills, one wheelwright shop, two sawmills, and two blacksmith shops in the whole area. Each of the five school districts making up the West End had a small school, and there was one hotel on the Hartford Road. The West End was a sparsely populated section of small to medium farms. Antioch, along Plainfield Pike, and Fountain Spring, which was on Greenville Avenue on the Smithfield-Johnston border, were the only locales approaching village status.

The northwest corner of the town has a granite marker where the four towns of Scituate, Glocester, Smithfield, and Johnston meet.

Today, the West End is the last rural area of town. A few farms remain, some industry has started along Plainfield Pike, and many stores have opened along Route 6. Basically, though, the West End remains rural with pockets of modern development.

Thought to have been built by the Reverend Samuel Winsor, this eighteenth-century house, pictured in the 1960s, is still lived in by his descendents. The house sits on a 150-acre farm off Winsor Avenue. Winsor, pastor of the First Baptist Church in Providence, broke off from that church and started his own Six Principle Church at Belknap in 1771. (Photograph courtesy of Carolyn Thornton.)

One of the heirs to the Reverend Samuel Winsor farm, John O. Winsor was born in 1842 on that farm, located off Winsor Avenue. He served in the Civil War, prospected for gold in Colorado, and bought out his nine brothers and sisters for the family estate. He later served in the state general assembly. (Photograph courtesy of Carolyn Thornton.)

Beautifully restored and maintained, this Winsor house stands at 29 Winsor Avenue. By 1851 this house was owned by an S. Winsor and it is thought that the second Reverend Samuel Winsor owned this land originally as part of his 1,000-acre farm.

The Israel Angell House, pictured in the 1950s, was located on Plainfield Pike in Johnston, near the Scituate border. It dated from the eighteenth century. It was moved from its original site when the extreme western part of Plainfield Pike was relocated in the nineteenth century. When the state widened the pike in the 1960s, the house was torn down. Angell, a colonel during the Revolution, lived in this house. (Photograph courtesy of Mohr Library.)

The Dean Kimball House, built in the mid-eighteenth century on Hopkins Avenue, was restored in the 1980s. An eighteenth-century barn was re-erected on the property. Kimball was one of the first councilmen in the town and his fine home reflects his wealth and status.

Now owned by the State of Rhode Island, the Dame Farm is operated as a farm museum. Located on Brown Avenue, this National Register site was occupied by the Steeres and later, the Dames, who still maintain the operation of the farm.

The Shang Bailey Tavern on Hartford Avenue in the western part of town was operated for many years as a hotel and tavern, first by the Cornell family and after by the Randall family. In the early part of this century Shang Bailey ran an infamous roadhouse here after a stint with the Barnum and Bailey Circus as "Shang the Chinese Giant." Today the Log Gift Shop is in business here.

Straddling the Smithfield-Johnston border just to the north of Greenville Avenue, this is the last remaining mill house from the Fountain Spring Mill. The ruins of the mill, dating to the late eighteenth and early nineteenth centuries, are nearby on the Smithfield side. One of the earliest textile machine factories in the country (and possibly the first) occupied the site around the turn of the eighteenth century.

Serving the southwest corner of Johnston, the Antioch School is located on the Plainfield Pike. It replaced an earlier school that burned in 1917. The building still stands, now used as a private residence. The photograph dates from the 1930s.

After the first chapel burned, the present Antioch Chapel on western Plainfield Pike was built in 1904. Pictured around 1915, it is typical of many small country churches. A thriving congregation meets here weekly. (Photograph courtesy of Joe Coduri.)

The Church of the Good Shepherd on Brown Avenue was burned by vandals in 1970. This mission church never had a full-time minister. Alva Carpenter, the minister from St. Peter's Episcopal Church, used to preach here Sunday afternoons in the early twentieth century. When necessary, lay people such as Stephen Clemence preached in the chapel. The church was built in 1886.

This tower of railroad ties was built for a 1939 Fourth of July bonfire at the Corsi farm on George Waterman Road. The tower is estimated to be 30 feet high.

The West End Station, constructed in 1955, serves the western section of the town and was the last of the four fire districts to have a firehouse. The truck pictured here was purchased from East Providence and was West End's first fire truck. Steven, son of Deputy Chief Eugene Frederick, is shown. (Photograph courtesy of Charles Redinger.)

Jenny's Tourist Home, photographed in 1938 at its Hartford Avenue location, advertised a "rest home atmosphere." Small overnight spots like this cropped up along our major highways to accommodate Americans on the move in their automobiles.

This small diner was run by Bob Larivee in the summer of 1958 on his property along Plainfield Pike west of Peck Hill Road. Business was not what he expected and he did not open the next year. (Photograph courtesy of Bob Larivee.)

Nine
Belknap

Belknap is a tiny village centered on Greenville Avenue at the terminus of Atwood Avenue. Its small size belies its importance to the town's history. Settlement goes back to at least the early 1700s when scattered farmhouses were built along the Killingly Road (now Greenville Avenue). The earliest recorded town meeting was held at the Benjamin Belknap House in 1759, and when the Reverend Samuel Winsor split from the First Baptist Church in Providence in 1771, it was to a meetinghouse in Belknap that he moved. The first Belknap school was built in 1790, probably the earliest in Johnston. Putting these events together, it becomes evident that Belknap was a center of town at that time.

Although there was a church, a school, and a store in the village, no industry ever developed. An 1803 map shows only a gristmill and what was probably a sawmill. An 1870 map shows only a blacksmith shop. Additionally, the Killingly Road never attained the importance of some other roads in town. Population thus remained low, and no important town buildings were ever located here.

Some early families were the Belknaps, the Mathewsons, the Thorntons, the Clemences, and the Crams.

An early- to mid-eighteenth-century home on Greenville Avenue, this house was owned by the Mathewson family for many years. The 1926 photograph shows Tommy Felding, a local handyman who rented the small, nineteenth-century cottage just west of this house. (Photograph courtesy of Elaine Pereira.)

Belknap, as shown on this 1870 map, is located on Greenville Avenue around the end of Atwood Avenue. Settlement goes back at least to the 1720s because houses were standing then on the Killingly Road (as Greenville Avenue was then known). Both a church and a school were built here in the last half of the eighteenth century.

Pictured about 1930, William Bruce Richardson stands with his dog in front of the Mathewson gambrel where he lived at the time. He entered the service as a naval officer during World War II and was killed in 1944 while aboard ship. (Photograph courtesy of Elaine Pereira.)

Job Belknap, pictured here in the 1870s, was born in 1837 in Belknap. He was the son of Emor and Mary (Lyon) Belknap and inherited the Benjamin Belknap House from them, living there all his life. Benjamin was his great-great grandfather. Job, his mother, and his grandmother (Esther Lyon) all had to work on the Belknap farm to get it into shape after years of neglect. (Photograph courtesy of Elaine Pereira.)

The Benjamin Belknap House on Greenville Avenue was purchased by Benjamin in 1741 and owned by his descendants until the 1960s. In 1759 the earliest recorded town meeting in Johnston was held here. Town meetings were rotated after that among a number of houses, this being one of them. The house was pretty much gutted in the 1960s and is in danger of being demolished. (Photograph courtesy of Phil Paige.)

A quiet moment in the yard of the Benjamin Belknap House at the corner of Greenville and Pine Hill Avenues is shown here. From left to right are Job Belknap, Emma (Job's daughter-in-law), unknown, Josie Belknap, Amy Belknap (Josie's sister), and unknown. (Photograph courtesy of Elaine Pereira.)

The Cram family poses in front of the giant oak tree on their property around the turn of the century. The tree was 26 feet around at the base. Their farm was west of Carpenter Drive, which runs from Atwood Avenue to Greenville Avenue. Stephen Thornton is said to have built the house.

Shown in 1909 or 1910, the students of the Belknap School pose with their teacher. The Belknap School still stands on Greenville Avenue, but no longer serves its original function. It served as a school from 1892 until about 1934. It replaced an earlier school on the site, which dated to 1790 and was used by subscribers. (Photograph courtesy of Elaine Pereira.)

This interior view of the Belknap School from 1924 presents a scene familiar in rural schools across Johnston and probably all across our country. (Photograph courtesy of Lora Clemence.)

Still standing on Greenville Avenue and still a church, the Belknap Chapel dates to 1891. It has always been run by the Industrial Society of Johnston, a group of local women. Affiliated in the early days with the Baptist church, in 1937 it adopted a non-denominational creed. The 1931 photograph shows automobiles parked outside the church for the Kaye wedding. (Photograph courtesy of Lora Clemence.)

Paris Mathewson, pictured about 1870, was born in 1804 and died an 1875. He was a horse dealer, a justice of the peace, sat on the probate court, served in the state general assembly, and was a gentleman farmer. He inherited the Mathewson Homestead after his father died and lived there the rest of his life. (Photograph courtesy of Elaine Mathewson Pereira.)

This scene from the 1890s looks west over the Mathewson Homestead farm on Greenville Avenue. William Mathewson's 1796 will mentions a store, a cooperage, and the house. A cooper, Mathewson's workplace shows just to the right of the house. To the right of that is a drive-through shed. On the left of the house is a blacksmith shop. On the north side of the road is the large store that had a hall on the second floor where dances and shows were held. (Photograph courtesy of Elaine Pereira.)

In the Mathewson family for over two hundred years, the Mathewson Homestead on Greenville Avenue was the center of a farm that included many outbuildings, among them a barn, a cooperage, a cider mill, a blacksmith shop, and a well house. Bought by William Mathewson in 1793, the farm remains a showplace. The house and a late-nineteenth-century barn behind it are left from the old days. (Photograph courtesy of Elaine Pereira.)

This cider house on the Mathewson Homestead farm was used for cider making in the early twentieth century. Located just to the east of the large store, it is now gone. (Photograph courtesy of Elaine Mathewson Pereira.)

A blacksmith shop on the Mathewson farm was situated on the south side of the road just to the east of the house. Any decent-sized farm was in constant need of a blacksmith. Many farmers did their own smithing, but the Mathewsons hired blacksmiths to work their shop. William H. Mathewson III tore the shop down when he was a young man. (Photograph courtesy of Elaine Pereira.)

Photographed in 1914 or 1915, this group all graduated from the eighth grade at the Manton School except for William H. Mathewson III. He is seated on the far left and was the only graduate from the Belknap School that year. They are all dressed to the nines! (Photograph courtesy of Elaine Mathewson Pereira.)

Bill Mathewson owned this delivery wagon and used it to deliver milk from his Greenville Avenue farm to area homes on Pine Hill. The delivery person is a young man named Joe and date of the photograph is c. 1915. (Photograph courtesy of Elaine Mathewson Pereira.)

The three men pictured here in the 1920s are haying on the Mathewson farm, probably on the north side of the road. On top of the pile of hay is William H. Mathewson III, in the middle is Richard F. Richardson (husband of Irene Mathewson), and on the left is a hired hand. (Photograph courtesy of Elaine Mathewson Pereira.)

Elaine Mathewson Pereira and her dad, William H. Mathewson III, were photographed about 1944 in front of the barn on the Mathewson farm. The barn remains, dating from the late nineteenth century with an addition from the 1920s. It looks just the same today as it did then. William kept about one hundred cows in this barn. He ran a dairy for awhile and was a dealer in livestock. (Photograph courtesy of Elaine Pereira.)

The original Mathewson Farm Equipment store on George Waterman Road is shown about 1947 or 1948. Melvin Bates is on the left and William H. Mathewson III is on the right. In the 1950s the business moved to a new building on the Mathewson farm on Greenville Avenue and is now run by William's son, Gibb Mathewson. (Photograph courtesy of Elaine Pereira.)

William H. Mathewson III is pictured driving a tractor on his farm in 1957. At this point the dairying and farming had ceased on the property, except for haying. (Photograph courtesy of Elaine Mathewson Pereira.)

Lora Clemence, pictured here about 1900 or 1905, was for many years a schoolteacher. She lived in Johnston for most of her adult life. The family home, the Stephen Clemence House, still stands at 475 Greenville Avenue, just east of the village school. Her children built a reproduction schoolhouse for her in the 1960s between the old school and her home. Used for a short time as a nursery, it is now a family-run watch repair shop. (Photograph courtesy of Lora Clemence.)

The convenience store comes to you! Blanchards's Traveling Store, shown in 1924, took care of country patrons before the widespread use of automobiles. The "store" is parked in front of the Stephen Clemence House, and the Clemence family made frequent use of this handy service. (Photograph courtesy of Lora Clemence.)

The Greenville Avenue Stables operated out of Stephen Clemence's barn on the south side of Greenville Avenue. Neighborhood children took riding lessons offered through the local 4-H Club. Lessons were given on Monday nights for 50¢ a session. Many of the youths participated in riding shows and demonstrations at local fairs, such as the Fiskeville Fair in Cranston. (Photograph courtesy of Lora Clemence.)

Gerald Clemence, son of Richard and Lora Clemence, plays the organ at the Belknap Church. As in most rural areas, the church here was not just the religious center but also the social and cultural center of the village. Numerous functions were held for church and village members such as suppers, 4-H and Sunday school activities, lectures, etc. (Photograph courtesy of Lora Clemence.)

Mary Clemence, sister of Richard R. Clemence, is pictured in 1929 inside the Belknap Church. She is practicing with some of the village children for a Mother's Day celebration. (Photograph courtesy of Lora Clemence.)

Photographed in 1929 on Greenville Avenue in front of the Stephen Clemence House, these siblings and friends are enjoying a quiet moment. Stephen (on the left) made this "machine" to haul things on the farm. It works well for his sister, Lora, too. Their brother Kenny is second from the right. Jennie and Lida (?) were friends. (Photograph courtesy of Lora Clemence.)

The fish was good—at least the cats thought so! The truck is stopped in front of the Stephen Clemence House in 1930. Many vendors traveled city and country roads selling their wares or services, including grinders, ragmen, ice wagons, and tinsmiths. (Photograph courtesy of Lora Clemence.)

This c. 1910 courting buggy belonged to the father of Lora Clemence, Richard R. Clemence, and looks more romantic than that '86 Escort. (Photograph courtesy of Lora Clemence.)

The Tri Mu, the local 4-H Club started by Lora E.O. Clemence and run by Clemence and Ethel Fassel in the 1920s and 1930s, poses outside the Belknap School. Tri Mu stood for Muscle, Mind, and Morals. (Photograph courtesy of Lora Clemence.)

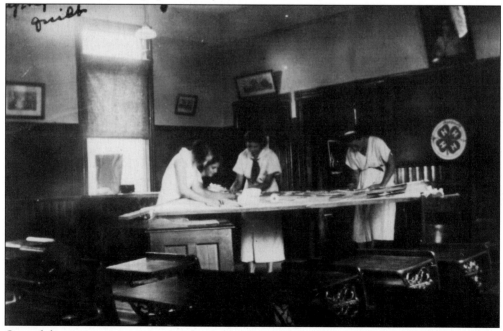

One of the numerous activities performed by the Tri Mu 4-H Club was the making of quilts. Young girls learned or practiced their sewing skills and socialized while doing it. The girls are pictured here in 1935 inside the village school. (Photograph courtesy of Lora Clemence.)

Ten
Olneyville-Merino

The Olneyville-Merino section is no longer a part of Johnston, but before its 1898 annexation to Providence it was the industrial, political, and population center of the town. Running from the western end of Olneyville Square to Neutaconkanut Hill and north to the Woonasquatucket River, this area produced Johnston's first textile mill, the Union Mill, and its first urban growth. The population of the section grew rapidly because of the mills and because it was the terminus of Plainfield, Hartford, and Manton Roads. By the mid-nineteenth century trains traveled through Olneyville, and its horse-drawn and electric trolleys were among the first in the metropolitan Providence area.

Numerous mills were built in Olneyville, some in Johnston, such as the Merino Mill, and some just across the river in Providence, such as the Atlantic Mills and the Providence and National Mills. Large numbers of workers were drawn to these mills and, by the late nineteenth century, Olneyville-Merino residents were clamoring for improved services (police, fire, water, etc.). At the same time residents of western Johnston were upset over the percentage of town taxes going to the upkeep of Olneyville-Merino. When a vote to annex the area came up in 1898, the Olneyville-Merino section was severed from Johnston.

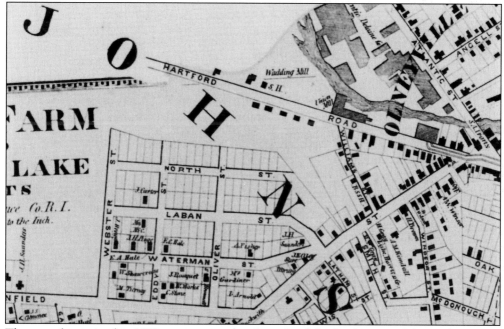

The area shown in this 1870 map encompassed much of the land annexed from Johnston to Providence in 1898. For 139 years, though, this section was an important part of Johnston with its large economic base and population.

The Providence-Johnston border ran down the Woonasquatucket River and then across the western side of Olneyville Square, shown here about 1900. Most of the buildings in the foreground were in Johnston including, on the left, Johnston's town hall. From 1870 to 1886 the town rented space for town offices in the Irons Block. (From R.L. Wonson Collection.)

The first Merino Mill was built in 1812 and burned in 1841. The second Merino Mill, pictured here, was erected in 1851 and for many years produced woolen goods. The building burned to the ground a few years ago.

Looking east toward Olneyville about 1915, the Odd Fellows Building (the brick building in the left-center of the photograph) at 161 Plainfield Street housed the Johnston Town Hall, probate court, jail, and police department from 1886 to 1898. The building no longer stands, but to many the junction of Plainfield Street and Pocasset Street is still Odd Fellows Square.

Notices such as these were posted around town by the town sergeant to announce town meetings. The town offices had moved to the Odd Fellows Block by this time, but town meetings were held in at least four sites in Olneyville in this period: Odd Fellows Hall, Wood's Hall and Irons' Hall (both in Olneyville Square), and the trolley car barn on Hartford Avenue. (Photograph courtesy of Providence City Hall Archives.)

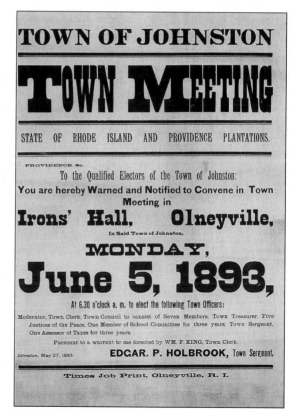

TOWN OF JOHNSTON
TOWN MEETING

STATE OF RHODE ISLAND AND PROVIDENCE PLANTATIONS.

PROVIDENCE. So.

To the Qualified Electors of the Town of Johnston:

You are hereby **Warned** and **Notified** to Convene in Town Meeting in

Irons' Hall, Olneyville,

In Said Town of Johnston,

MONDAY,
June 5, 1893,

At 6.30 o'clock a. m. to elect the following Town Officers:

Moderator, Town Clerk, Town Council to consist of Seven Members, Town Treasurer, Five Justices of the Peace, One Member of School Committee for three years, Town Sergeant, One Assessor of Taxes for three years.

Pursuant to a warrant to me directed by WM. F. KING, Town Clerk.

Johnston, May 27, 1893.　　　　**EDGAR. P. HOLBROOK**, Town Sergeant.

Times Job Print, Olneyville, R. I.

The Select School, pictured in about 1885, was in Olneyville. The four children of George F. and Abby L. (Angell) Beane are in the group. William H. is in the front row, first on the left. Louisa A. and Josephine A. are the second and fourth ones from the left in the second row. G. Frederic is the baby in his mother's arms in the doorway. (Photograph courtesy of Evelyn Beaumier.)

Olneyville, because of its mills and large population, had trolley service very early, with horse-drawn trolleys present in 1865. This trolley barn is on lower Hartford Avenue just out of Olneyville Square. It still stands. Note that the driver stands outside the main compartment of the car, exposed to the elements. Hopefully he dressed in layers! (Photograph courtesy of Scott Molloy.)

Because of its large population and its many businesses, Olneyville had an early need for good fire protection. The Rough & Ready Station, the first in Johnston, was built in 1891 at the corner of Plainfield and Rye Streets. The Rough & Ready Eagle #2 Fire Company, though, goes back to 1886 when the volunteer group was formed under foreman Samuel E. Groves.

This is the burial site of Governor Samuel Ward King, Johnston's only governor. The cemetery is on Hartford Avenue at the corner of Winfield Street, diagonally across from the King Homestead. King was governor during the Dorr War when Rhode Island had two elected governors. He was declared the legal one. This and the following six sites are all in Johnston, but close to the annexed area.

This soapstone quarry, a National Register site, is located just off Hartford Avenue a short distance west of Killingly Street. The site was worked by Indians who fashioned bowls and possibly other implements from the soft rock. Another soapstone quarry is located in Cranston, but these sites are uncommon in New England. The photograph was taken in the 1960s.

The Ochee Springs Bottling Company was situated on the same property as the soapstone quarry. The company made soft drinks for much of this century, using a fine local spring for its water. The Colorlith Company has built around part of the old Ochee Springs building. The fire took place in the 1940s. (Photograph courtesy of Manton Hose Co. #3.)

The Providence & Danielson Railroad was an interurban trolley line that operated between its namesake cities. It traveled the length of Johnston, roughly following the Hartford Pike most of the way. The P&D waiting station and store, shown here in a postcard view, were across the street from the car barn on Hartford Avenue. At the time of this picture it was called E.F. Pratt's. Later it was Sweet's Store.

The Providence & Danielson car barn, still standing, is located on the south side of Hartford Avenue, just west of Killingly Street. Drivers would switch cars at this point after the ride in from Danielson, and a new set of drivers would take the car to Providence. The P&D also hauled freight such as milk from the country and, in turn, brought goods to rural areas from the city. It ceased operations in the 1920s.

The Franklin School is pictured here in the early twentieth century. Jennie Antonelli, a local resident, stands in the front of the scene. The school was just south of Hartford Avenue and west of Winfield Street. Students would go here for grades one through six and then would go to Calef Junior High in the Manton section, many having to walk a couple of miles each way. (Photograph courtesy of Catherine Iozzi.)

This is the Joshua Greene House (1710), given to him by his father-in-law, John Manton. It descended through the family to the Tourtellotts, who were the last people to live here before the house was moved to Woodstock, Connecticut (1995). Pictured are Zeke Potter on the left and David A. and Mary Elizabeth Tourtelott on the right. The names of the two men sitting to Zeke's left are unknown. (Photograph courtesy of Jack Mearon.)